"**I've bought books that made me think. This one made me act.** A must-read for leaders and anyone who touches the customer."

— Adam Unger,CEO at Accutech Systems

"**think/WOW is a fun, fast read packed with lessons for leaders and frontline teams alike.** Its engaging vignettes reveal simple, powerful behaviors that create unforgettable customer moments"

— Bob Kraut,Board Member & Advisor,Former CMO,Papa John s

"**think/WOW is a masterclass in customer experience**—blending the visionary spark of Tom Peters' Pursuit of Wow with the practical punch of the Knock Your Socks Off series. It's a blueprint for inspiring loyalty, sparking joy, and exceeding expectations. I'm ready to put these tactics to work immediately."

— Blake Holman,AI & Leadership Evangelist

"Separately, 'think' and 'WOW' are powerful. Together, they're transformational. At their intersection lies the performance magic that elevates teams and businesses. **Daren delivers a clear blueprint for bringing that magic to every client and employee experience.**"

— Bruce Sammis,Former CEO,Lockton Dunning

think/WOW: Exceptional Customer Experience

Cover, Interior Design and Illustrations by the very talented Mama Daniel.

Printed in PRC.
ISBN: 978-1-968127-11-4

THE GOAL AS A COMPANY IS TO HAVE CUSTOMER SERVICE THAT IS NOT JUST THE BEST BUT LEGENDARY.

— **Sam Walton**

THE CUSTOMER EXPERIENCE IS THE NEXT COMPETITIVE BATTLEGROUND.

— **Jerry Gregoire**

THE KEY IS WHEN A CUSTOMER WALKS AWAY THINKING, 'WOW, I LOVE DOING BUSINESS WITH THEM, AND I WANT TO TELL OTHERS ABOUT THE EXPERIENCE.

— **Shep Hyken**

DEDICATED TO THE SPECTACULAR ELISE. YOU HAVE BEEN BRINGING ME WOW SINCE THE MOMENT I MET YOU.

CUSTOMERS DESCRIBING THEIR SERVICE EXPERIENCE AS "SUPERIOR" = 8%

COMPANIES
DESCRIBING
THEIR CUSTOMER'S
EXPERIENCE
"SUPERIOR" = 80%*

*Study by Bain and Company Survey 362 companies. In Tom Peters book The Excellence Dividend

MOST BUSINESSES ARE

BORING

MUNDANE
THE SAME **TYPICAL**
YAWN MEHHH...

WE SNOOZE
YOU LOSE.

WE LIVE IN A PROSE FLATTENED WORLD.

Walter Brueggemann

Life is extraordinary.

We were created for greatness.

It's time to wake up out of our slumber and bring the **WOW**.

It's time to put the poetry back in every encounter, moment, and experience.

10

Have you ever had a customer service experience or encounter with a company that was …

**SO UNIQUE,
SO CONSISTENT,
SO AMAZING,**

that all you could say was ▷

WOW Service is … Doing even ordinary things with extraordinary attention thus evoking a "**WOW!**"

WHERE WOW LIVES

Every single day, every project you work on, every meeting you attend, every personal encounter, and every customer interaction is an opportunity to deliver WOW.

WOW LIVES IN
- ☑ big money savings
- ☑ value added deliverables
- ☑ jaw dropping new products

WOW LIVES IN SIMPLE THINGS LIKE ...

- ☑ the speed of a return call
- ☑ the way something is packaged
- ☑ a creative idea freely offered
- ☑ attentive listening
- ☑ making eye contact.

THE NUMBER ONE INDICATOR OF SUCCESS WAS ...

NOT if you solved their problem
NOT how quickly you solved their problem
NOT how they felt about you ...

GREAT CUSTOMER EXPERIENCE BOILED DOWN TO ONE THING ...
How they felt about **THEMSELVES** following the encounter.

THINK ABOUT IT. YOU CALL I.T. SUPPORT AND TELL THEM YOUR ISSUE.

I.T. SUPPORT: "DO YOU SEE THE BIG GREEN BUTTON." THE VOICE ON THE OTHER END GROANS CONDESCENDINGLY.

YOU: "YES"

I.T. SUPPORT: "PUSH IT"

YOU: "WHOA, THAT FIXED IT."

I.T. SUPPORT: "IT WAS AN 'ID-10-T PROBLEM'." HE SCOFFS.

YOU: "THAT SOUNDS BAD, WHAT IS THAT?"

I.T. SUPPORT: "WRITE IT OUT HE SAYS" HANGING UP ON YOU.

YOUR ISSUE WAS COMPLETELY ADDRESSED IN LESS THAN 60 SECONDS. IN THE PROCESS THE TECH MADE YOU FEEL LIKE A LOSER AND CALLED YOU AN "IDIOT".

"CUSTOMER EXPERIENCE IS MORE THAN WHAT WE DELIVER, IT'S HOW WE MAKE CUSTOMERS FEEL."

Shep Hyken

In the following pages we are going to look at ideas, strategies, tactics and more for how you can bring **WOW** to every encounter and experience with both internal and external customers.

Most businesses are sleepwalking through customer service. But not yours. Because you're about to wake up, spark joy, and **WOW** them in ways they've never seen.

THINK!

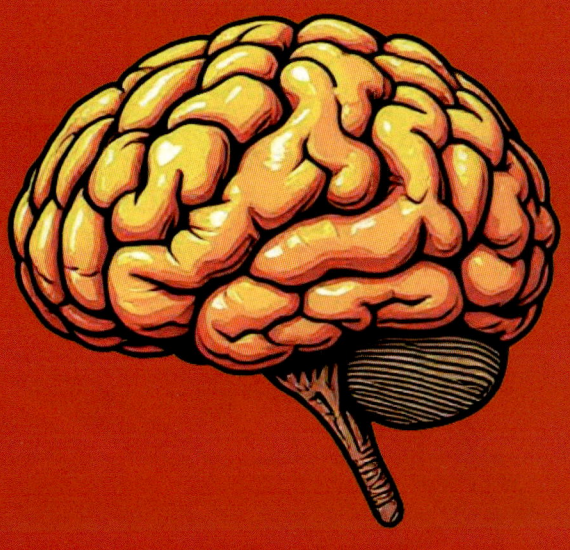

"THERE'S NO SUBSTITUTE FOR THINKING"

Dave Lamp, CEO

THOUGHTFULNESS IN EVERY INTERACTION

HUMAN CONNECTION THAT CREATES LASTING IMPRESSIONS

IMMEDIACY IN RESOLVING ISSUES

NURTURING LOYALTY AND TRUST

KNOWING YOUR CUSTOMER

21

THE POWER OF A SINGLE WORD

In 1911, Thomas J. Watson was a sales manager at National Cash Register. During a meeting, frustrated by the lack of mental engagement, he stopped mid-discussion and said,

"The trouble with most of us is we don't think enough. We're not paid for our feet—we're paid for our heads."

He walked to the chalkboard and wrote one word in big letters: **THINK**.

That one word became his personal mantra—and later, a corporate revolution.

When Watson took over the Computing-Tabulating-Recording Company (which became IBM) in 1914, he brought **THINK** with him. Soon, the word appeared on signs in offices, factories, and meeting rooms worldwide.

It wasn't just decoration—it was a call to action. **THINK** became IBM's rallying cry for innovation, intelligence, and solving problems before they happened.

From one inspired moment in a sales meeting, **THINK** became a philosophy that shaped one of the most influential companies in history.

22

BEER COASTER

In the late 1980's I, Bruce Sammis, was at a happy hour late in the week. A group of what looked like 30 somethings all dressed alike (suits, white shirts, ties,.....) was celebrating completing several days of training before they caught flights home. As the drinks flowed, they got louder and more disruptive, they were excited but clearly headed off the conduct cliff. I was watching the train going off the tracks and for once I was not on the train.

Suddenly an older businessman approached the group and dropped a bar coaster on their table. No words were spoken, he was gone as quickly as he emerged. Instantly a wave of sobriety overcame the group. The singing, yelling and rounds of shots stopped. The group paid their tab said their goodbyes and headed to the airport. Train back on the tracks, crisis averted.

I walked over to the empty table looking for the coaster that saved the 30 somethings from embarrassment or more serious consequences. In the middle of the table was a coaster with one word written in ink **"THINK"**.   These IBM employees immediately understood.

24

GREAT CUSTOMER EXPERIENCE EMERGES WHEN YOU ENCOURAGE, INSIST ON, AND EMPOWER YOUR EMPLOYEES TO THINK.

A thinking employee can solve many issues in an effective and efficient manner rather than just reciting the company policy.

You know it is not a thinking culture when you hear phrases like …

- ☑ **THERE IS NOTHING I CAN DO …**
- ☑ **OUR POLICY STATES …**
- ☑ **WE ARE REQUIRED TO …**

OR, when someone can't abandon the script no matter how badly the situation calls for it.

I walked into my favorite chicken spot and looked at the 3-piece special.

ME: "INSTEAD OF A BREAST AND TWO WINGS CAN I JUST GET THREE WINGS?"

EMPLOYEE: "I AM SORRY SIR; WE DON'T ALLOW SUBSTITUTIONS."

ME: ???

The reason for that policy is to prevent people swapping less expensive pieces of meat for more expensive and thus cutting into the profit margin.

The restaurant would actually make money on my "substitution" and if the owner had been waiting on me, he would have gladly made that trade.

IT IS OUR POLICY

BEST BUY

Years ago, I walked into Best Buy with a sealed DVD of a concert performance of one of my all-time favorite bands, U2.

I had discovered that the one I bought for $16.99 was the basic version and I wanted the deluxe version for $24.95.

I located the more expensive version I wanted and brought both to the customer service line and waited my turn.

Finally, I was called to the counter and explained the following …

ME: "I BOUGHT THIS BASIC VERSION A FEW MONTHS AGO AND HAVE NEVER OPENED IT. I WANT TO EXCHANGE IT FOR THE DELUXE VERSION AND WILL HAPPILY PAY THE DIFFERENCE."

EMPLOYEE: "DO YOU HAVE A RECEIPT?"

ME: "I DO NOT."

EMPLOYEE: "I'M SORRY BUT I CAN'T EXCHANGE IT WITHOUT A RECEIPT."

ME: "YOU KNOW THE STORE IS GOING TO MAKE ADDITIONAL MONEY ON THIS TRANSACTION."

EMPLOYEE: "IT'S OUR POLICY."

ME: "IS THERE ANYTHING WE CAN DO TO CHANGE THAT?"

EMPLOYEE: "WOULD YOU LIKE TO SPEAK TO THE MANAGER?"

ME: "SURE!"

After some friendly discussion with the clerk, *(never be a jerk to people who are working for a living – or anyone else for that matter)* the manager arrived.

Upon hearing the clerk describe the situation, he looked at her with an astonished look and said,

"ABSOLUTELY. DO IT."

The problem was not an "incompetent employee".

THE PROBLEM WAS, SHE HAD NOT BEEN EMPOWERED TO THINK.

POLICY: NO SUBSTITUTIONS.

PRINCIPLE: DO WHATEVER MAKES THE COMPANY MONEY.

POLICY: NO EXCEPTIONS.*

PRINCIPLE: MAKE REASONABLE EXCEPTIONS WHICH BENEFIT THE BUSINESS AND THE CUSTOMER.

POLICY: ONLY A MANAGER IS ALLOWED TO MAKE THAT DECISION.

PRINCIPLE: TEACH EVERY EMPLOYEE HOW TO THINK LIKE A MANAGER AND EMPOWER THEM TO ACT.

I REMEMBER HEARING ABOUT AN HONOR STUDENT SENT HOME FOR HAVING A WEAPON BECAUSE SHE BROUGHT A BUTTER KNIFE TO SCHOOL TO SLICE THE APPLE IN HER LUNCH. THE SCHOOL HAD A "ZERO WEAPONS" POLICY.

35

TRAIN YOUR TEAM TO BE PROBLEM SOLVERS NOT POLICY PLODDERS.

BRAVO TRADER JOES!"

I pulled my buggy up to the register at my local Trader Joes with several boxes of wine and some snack food.

TEAM MEMBER: "YOU MUST BE HAVING SOME KIND OF PARTY!"

ME: "ACTUALLY I AM GETTING MARRIED IN MY CONDO TODAY AND THIS IS FOR THE AFTER PARTY!"

TEAM MEMBER: "REALLY?! THAT IS SO EXCITING!"

She then ran off saying, "I'll be right back." Moments later she returned with a large bouquet of flowers and said, "This is for the happy couple."

41

I was blown away. I went to my car, put the groceries away, grabbed several copies of my WSJ & USA Today bestseller A Company of Owners and went back in the store.

I brought the books to the manager and told him what a great job his team was doing and then I said this to him …

"WHAT JUST HAPPENED IS NOT ONLY A REFLECTION OF A GREAT EMPLOYEE, BUT IT ALSO REPRESENTS AMAZING MANAGEMENT AND AN INCREDIBLE COMPANY.

YOU HAVE BUILT A COMPANY WHERE YOUR TEAM MEMBER WAS EMPOWERED TO ACT ON HER OWN TO DO SOMETHING COOL WITHOUT GETTING PERMISSION OR WORRYING IF SHE WOULD BE IN TROUBLE.

BRAVO TRADER JOES!"

RITZ-CARLTON $2,000 RULE

The Ritz-Carlton provides employees with the authority to spend up to $2,000 per guest, per incident to resolve any issues with prior approval from a manager. **think/WOW** is about purposeful planned action that provides value.

THE RITZ-CARLTON

CONSUELO GOES TO HAWAII

A businessman was staying at the Ritz. On his last day he headed to the airport to fly to Hawaii for his next event. On his way to the plane, he realized he had forgotten his computer at the hotel! There was not time to head back and get it, so he called the Ritz and told them the dilemma and that he absolutely had to have it by the next day at 3 o'clock for his very important presentation. "I don't care what it costs but can you please get it to me!" he pleaded.

The GM of the hotel walked in the next day and casually enquired,

GM: "WHERE'S CONSUELO?"

THE TEAM: "CONSUELO FLEW OUT LAST NIGHT ON THE RED EYE TO HAWAII."

GM: "WHY?"

The team told him about the left computer and said, "She did not trust the delivery services to be able to get it there on time, so she took the computer to Hawaii."

You may be thinking, "Oh, yeah, Consuelo just wanted to go to Hawaii."

Nope. She went to Hawaii, delivered the computer, went straight back to the airport, and flew home.

WHEN SHE ARRIVED BACK AT THE RITZ THE ENTIRE TEAM INCLUDING THE GM GAVE HER A STANDING OVATION.

45

EMPOWER YOUR TEAM TO MAKE QUICK DECISIONS THAT DELIGHT CUSTOMERS WITHOUT NEEDING TO ASK FOR PERMISSION.

WOW doesn't typically happen by accident.

WOW comes from strategic and creative thinking about how to provide above and beyond value.

think/WOW is about getting the right kind of **WOWs**.

☑ I can't believe you did that
☑ How wonderful
☑ What incredible service
☑ Awesome, Amazing, Spectacular
☑ I've never had anyone do that before
☑ That was so thoughtful
☑ For me, really?
☑ **WOW!**

WOW PREPARATION

GREAT WOWS ARE THE RESULT OF THOUGHTFUL PREPARATION, CREATIVE THINKING, AND INTENTIONAL DELIVERY.

THOUGHTFUL PREPARATION

IT'S HARD TO PULL OFF A LAST-MINUTE WOW.

If you are sitting in a lobby trying to figure out how to bring the **WOW** in a meeting that starts in 2 minutes, good luck.

It will be a challenge to come up with something that doesn't require at least a little preparation.

EXCEPTION: IF YOU PRACTICE THIS BRAIN "MUSCLE" OF CREATING **WOW** ON OCCASION AN IDEA MAY COME TO YOU SPONTANEOUSLY.

I provided a Keynote Talk for a large hotel group in Dallas, TX. The CEO opened the annual event. With music blaring he ran onstage, there was a "Boom", and confetti rained down on him. The team broke out in massive applause.

Following his talk, I asked my assistant to gather up as much of the confetti as she could.

The next day when I was introduced by the CEO, I came on stage and said this.

"I NEED THE CEO TO COME BACK UP HERE."

Once he was back by my side, I continued …

"WHEN THE CEO WAS INTRODUCED TO SPEAK THERE WAS MUCH FANFARE INCLUDING A SHOWER OF CONFETTI. I WANT AN APPROXIMATION OF THAT WELCOME."

I then handed the CEO the bucket of the recovered confetti.

"LET'S DO THIS OVER. MR. CEO, PLEASE INTRODUCE ME AGAIN AND WHEN I COME ON STAGE, DUMP THIS BUCKET OF CONFETTI ON MY HEAD. "

He did. The crowd went wild, and we were off to a great start.

Following the talk he remarked, "You get us, and I want you to come back next year!"
WOW!

ENCOURAGE WOW IDEAS BOTH PLANNED AND SPONTANEOUS. CELEBRATE AND REWARD THOSE WHO MAKE THEM HAPPEN.

CREATIVE THINKING

☑ **ALL** PEOPLE CAN BE CREATIVE.

☑ **EVERYONE** CAN DEVELOP CREATIVITY AS A SKILL BY PRACTICING THE ART OF CREATIVE THINKING.

☑ CREATIVE THINKING LIVES IN **QUESTION MARKS** NOT PERIODS.

☑ CREATIVE THINKING ABOUT CUSTOMER SERVICE

WOW COMES FROM ASKING QUESTIONS LIKE

- ☑ WHAT DO CUSTOMERS LIKE?
- ☑ WHAT DO CUSTOMERS NEED?
- ☑ WHAT WOULD I WANT IF I WERE IN THEIR SHOES?
- ☑ WHAT WOULD BLOW MY CUSTOMERS AWAY?
- ☑ HOW CAN I MAKE THEIR EXPERIENCE TRULY "**WOW**"?

ACT:

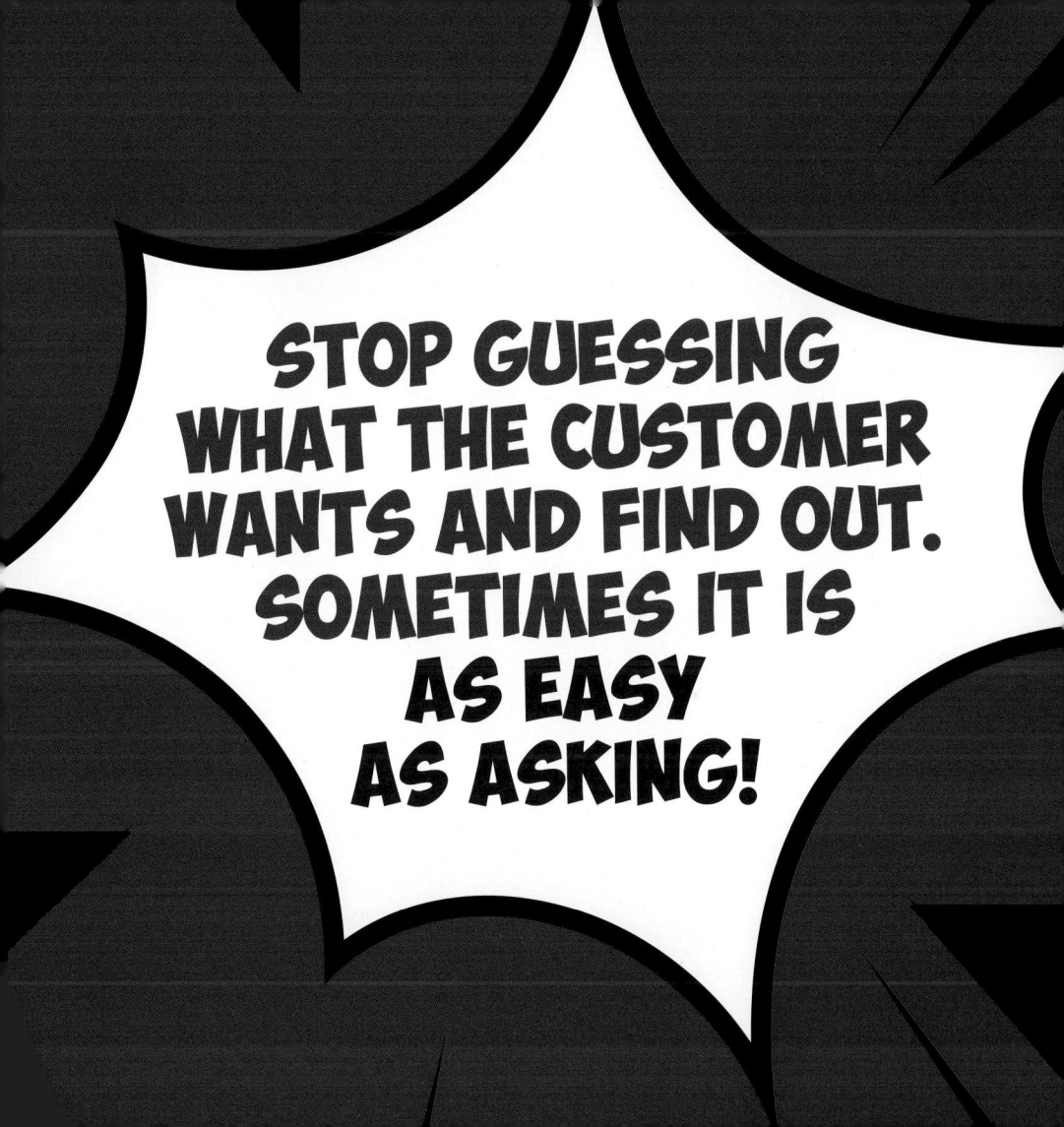

WOW

W.O.W. – WATCH, OWN, WIN

W – WATCH FOR OPPORTUNITIES

WOW moments come from being attentive and actively seeking opportunities to exceed expectations. It's about being observant and always asking, "Where can I add value and delight my customer?"

Small details matter, and anticipating needs before they're voiced is key to **WOW** moments.

O — OWN THE EXPERIENCE

Take full responsibility for every customer interaction. Whether it's resolving an issue, creating a special moment, or simply being there to assist, ownership* is key to creating **WOW**.

If a problem arises, own it from start to finish—even if it wasn't your fault. Customers want to feel like someone has their back.

W — WIN THEIR LOYALTY - WHATEVER IT TAKES

WOW happens when you're willing to go the extra mile. It's the willingness to think creatively, break away from routine, and offer something extraordinary.

Whether that's staying late to solve a problem or making an extra effort to personalize a customer's experience, **WOW** means doing What Others Won't.

Strive to exceed what the customer expects, every time. It's not enough to meet their needs— aim to **WOW** them by delivering more than they imagined.

WOW THEM BY DELIVERING MORE THAN THEY IMAGINED.

IT IS EASY TO GET A WOW.

THERE ARE MANY WAYS TO GET A WOW ...

▷ Walk out in the middle of a crowd and set your hair on fire.

▷ Say something really inappropriate and offensive

▷ Just flat out don't deliver

▷ Have sucky products in sucky packaging delivered with a sucky attitude

ALL THESE THINGS WOULD PRODUCE A "WOW"! BUT NOT THE KIND YOU WANT.

WOW KILLERS

- [x] Something you ordered at the drive through is not in the bag when you get home.
- [x] The product is much shoddier than the description or pictures conveyed.
- [x] You spend 30 minutes just getting the product out of the package.
- [x] You spend 5 hours following poorly written or illustrated instructions to try and put something together
- [x] It breaks
- [x] It doesn't work
- [x] You are treated poorly
- [x] You stand in line forever

WOW THRILLERS

- ☑ Early delivery
- ☑ Great packaging
- ☑ Value added
- ☑ Bells and whistles
- ☑ Free stuff
- ☑ Life application
- ☑ Unselfish act
- ☑ Remembering preferences
- ☑ A gift
- ☑ It's easier
- ☑ It's intuitive
- ☑ Extras thrown in
- ☑ Amazing service

WOW IS ...

👉 Bringing value to another person.
👉 Pleasantly surprising them.
👉 Doing something unique and different (or even ordinary) in a way that evokes a

WOWING CUSTOMERS

"Think WOW! There is (absolutely, positively) no reason why professional service firms should not … as a matter of course … be about WOW!

"Simple point: Why the hell bother to get out of bed in the morning if your objective is not … WOW! Or: Holy Maloney! Or: Neat! Or: Over the top!

"These are precisely the terms that should apply to the completion of any project … at Accounting, Inc. … Purchasing, Inc. … Marketing, Inc. … Design, Inc. … Apparel Inc., whatever … whoever … wherever … whenever."

— Tom Peters,
The Circle of Innovation
(The King of Wow!)

YOU ARE WALKING INTO ONE OF THESE PLACES.

THE BANK | A CASINO | YOUR CABLE COMPANY | A SPEAK EASY RUN BY HIPSTERS |

SHINOLA

NORDSTROM

TARGET

UNITED STATES POSTAL SERVICE

DO YOU EXPECT A GREAT CUSTOMER EXPERIENCE OR A FRUSTRATING TEDIOUS CUSTOMER EXPERIENCE?

WHY?

ARE YOUR RESPONSES BASED ON PERSONAL EXPERIENCE, PERCEPTION, OR PEOPLE'S COMMENTARY?

WE WANT

PASSIONATE FANS.

Customers will only be as excited about you and your services as **YOU** are excited about you and your services.

Customers will only be as excited about you as you are about **THEM**.

BIG MISTAKES:

☑ Adopting an us/them mentality

☑ **Not** inviting customers behind the curtain

☑ **Not** knowing what your customers love and care about

☑ Employees who only work at your company because they need a J-O-B. (They do not represent you well.)

WHEN YOU WORK FOR A COMPANY OR BUSINESS, YOU ARE A
BRAND AMBASSADOR

IF SOMEONE IS RUDE TO YOU IN AN AIRPORT YOU SAY,

"WHAT A RUDE PERSON."

IF A FLIGHT ATTENDANT IS RUDE TO YOU ON THE PLANE YOU SAY,

"WHAT A RUDE AIRLINE!"

BRING THE WOW:

Get up in the morning excited about the opportunity to **WOW** today

WOW is a calling
WOW is a passion
WOW is a lifestyle

WOW is about playing full out and delivering everything you do at a level that mesmerizes and astounds.

See innovation and **WOW** as a MAJOR part of your VALUE.

Providing **WOW** is what separates you from the pack.

It makes you THE Market Leader.

WOW PUNCHES HOLES IN THE MUNDANE AND CREATES A MEMORABLE EXPERIENCE.

RETAIL IS NOT DEAD!

BORING RETAIL IS DEAD!

MICHAEL KORS

My wife is a big fan. Her sister told her they could get their Michael Kors bags for a discount at the outlet mall just outside of Dallas. So, one Saturday morning, off they went.

My wife rummaged through the piled-up bags, picked out one she liked, and headed to the long line at the counter. She was horrified to see the clerks dumping the bags unceremoniously into a paper bag and sending the shoppers on their way.

She also noticed that these bags were not like the ones sold in the mall store. They were missing the lining and several other details that made the bags special.

She tossed aside her intended purchase and headed off to the mall store. Here is the account in her own words.

"They sat me down and brought me champagne. They set out to match the bags to my needs and my coloring.

'What will you carry in the bag the woman said?'

'How often will you use this particular bag?' the woman asked.

Then she showed me the perfect bag and I bought it. They took the time to know my needs and treat me like I was the only customer that mattered.

Eliseism – **'Treat every guest like you are receiving royalty'.**

They treated me like I was royalty even though they knew nothing about me. The experience was worth more than the money I spent on the bag which I used daily for four years."

WOW SURPRISES

My incredible daughter Callahan was having a rough day. She dragged into the kitchen looking like the world had just ended.

I said, "sweetie, I am so sorry you are having a rough day. You know, sometimes the best therapy is just to break something!"

I grabbed a (plastic) wine glass off the island and threw it between her feet. The look of shock and fear as she watched the "glass" accelerate to instant shatter was only surpassed by the startled laughter that erupted from her when …

THE GLASS BOUNCED.

PROVIDE EXTRA ...

FUN
SPEED
DESIGN
VALUE
BEAUTY
INTRIGUE
PIZZAZZ
PEPPERONI
FEATURES
SAVINGS
STUFF
FLAIR
COOL
EASE

STANDARDIZE YOUR WOW!

TO HAVE A TRUE THINK/WOW COMPANY IT NEEDS TO BE CONSISTENT ACROSS PEOPLE, PLACES, AND PROCESSES.

Having one great customer service provider at one location just sets customers up for disappointment when they don't receive the same kind of service from a different location or person.

CONSISTENCY CREATES TRUST … WOW OVER AND OVER AGAIN

CONSISTENCY *NOT* AUTHENTICITY

People don't care about authenticity at all; they care about consistency.

— **Seth Godin**

People don't want an authentic lawyer, an authentic entertainer, an authentic surgeon, an authentic deli shop. We want a **CONSISTENT** one. You want the best version of that person, regardless of if they are in a bad mood or not*.

— **Seth Godin**

*A Productive Conversation with Mike Vardy, Episode 343

> *Whether it is his 21 bestselling books, his daily blog, AltMBA, Akimbo Workshops and all of the other things he creates, Seth Godin models consistency.*

When it comes to Customer Experience people want consistency NOT authenticity. When someone has a great experience at your store, service, hotel, restaurant … they get excited and want to come back! It was exceptional.

IF they return eager for a repeat performance and this time none of the magic is there … they recoil in frustration proclaiming to themselves and worse, maybe others, "I knew they couldn't keep it up". AND, they write you off and don't come back.

JOE'S STONE CRAB – MIAMI, FL

I absolutely love the stone crab at Joe's in Miami. When it is in season and I am there, it is a total destination for me. Family-run for over 100 years, famous for not taking reservations yet still delivering flawless service. Regulars know exactly what to expect—right down to the crispness of the coleslaw and the warmth of the key lime pie. A manager once said: "People come for the crab, but they come back for the certainty."

"HOSPITALITY WITHOUT CONSISTENCY
IS A BROKEN PROMISE,"

— Danny Meyer

"IF YOU'RE NOT CONSISTENT, YOU'RE
NOT DEPENDABLE. AND IF YOU'RE
NOT DEPENDABLE, YOU'RE NOT
DELIVERING SERVICE—YOU'RE JUST
ROLLING DICE."

— Barbara Glanz

"WITHOUT CONSISTENCY,
EXCELLENCE IS IRRELEVANT."

— Horst Schulze, Co-Founder of Ritz-Carlton

"ONE-OFF MAGIC IS NICE. REPEATABLE
MAGIC IS WHAT BUILDS A BUSINESS. IF
YOU CAN'T DO IT AGAIN TOMORROW,
IT'S NOT GOOD SERVICE—IT'S JUST
LUCK."

— Ari Weinzweig, Zingerman's Deli

WOW moments aren't just one-off surprises—they should be built into your everyday operations so that customers can expect excellence every time.

Develop systems that ensure consistent, high-quality service across all touchpoints. Audit your customer experience regularly to make sure WOW moments are sustainable.

THE WOW FUN ZONE

IT IS DIFFICULT FOR TEAM MEMBERS TO FOCUS ON PROVIDING WOW WHEN THEY ARE MIRED DOWN BY BROKEN EQUIPMENT, TEDIOUS PROCESSES, BUREAUCRATIC HINDRANCES, AND MORE.

SOUTHWEST®

In the early days, one of the reasons Southwest Airlines was viewed as such a "fun" airline is because they were fastidious about making their processes work.

For gate agents, flight attendants and other team members, it is easier to be in a great mood when you are not constantly dealing with problems and late flights.

97

FREE YOUR TEAM UP TO FOCUS ON WOW BY REMOVING UNNECESSARY ENCUMBRANCES TO THEIR WORK.*

*I wrote a whole book about the myriads of these. It is Called Unbeach your Company: Learning to Swim in the New Ocean.

HIRE *WOW!*

WOW does not happen by accident. Hiring people with a **WOW** attitude is vital.

I understand that a very successful and well-run fast food chain vets interviewees in the following manner:

WHILE TALKING, THE INTERVIEWER "ACCIDENTLY" KNOCKS SOME PAPERS OFF THE DESK.

IF THE INTERVIEWEE QUICKLY LEANS OVER TO HELP PICK THEM UP, THEY SURVIVE ROUND ONE.

IF THE INTERVIEWEE JUST SITS THERE WHILE THE INTERVIEWER PICKS THE PAPERS UP, THEY ARE NOT GETTING THE JOB.

INTERVIEW IDEAS FOR HIRING *WOW*

☑ Watch how they treat servers at a lunch interview.

☑ Leave them in a room with an obvious mess on the table and see if they clean it up.

☑ Ask them about their favorite businesses and what they love about them.

☑ Have them brainstorm ways to create more **WOW** at your company. See if the ideas flow.

☑ Have the server at a lunch interview bring them the wrong meal and see how they respond.

GREAT BUSINESSES LIKE ...

BAKE THE WOW INTO THEIR SYSTEM SO
THAT IT IS CONSISTENT NO MATTER WHERE YOU
ARE OR WITH WHOM YOU ARE DEALING.

WOW must be FOUNDATIONAL to the culture of your COMPANY both **INTERNAL** and **EXTERNAL**.

MAKE WOW A PART OF YOUR COMPANY ETHOS!

(ETHOS – THE CHARACTERISTIC SPIRIT OF A CULTURE.)

WOW isn't just for customers. It's for your team too. When you hire **WOW**-minded people, you create a culture that mirrors that same energy internally.

If you want your employees to **WOW** customers, start by **WOWing** them.

TIE THE WOW CULTURE BACK INTO TEAM EMPOWERMENT AND HIRING:

WOW GIFTS

IN LOUISIANA, THEY CALL IT "LAGNIAPPE".

IN THAILAND, THEY CALL IT "TAM FREE".

BUDDHISTS CALL IT THE "PARAMITA OF DANA" (THE PERFECTION OF CHARITY)*

IN FINE DINING IT IS CALLED "AMUSE-BOUCHE"

Everyone likes something extra.

WHEN YOU GIVE SOMETHING ABOVE AND BEYOND, PEOPLE FEEL APPRECIATED AND SPECIAL.

*from The Dharma Bums, Jack Kerouac

World class restaurants will often deliver a sample of something you did not order with a comment like, "the Chef wanted you to try her new creation …" Revolution in New Orleans is great at this!

This is a double bonus because not only is it unexpected, but it is also from the chef.

Here is a simple but powerful rule.

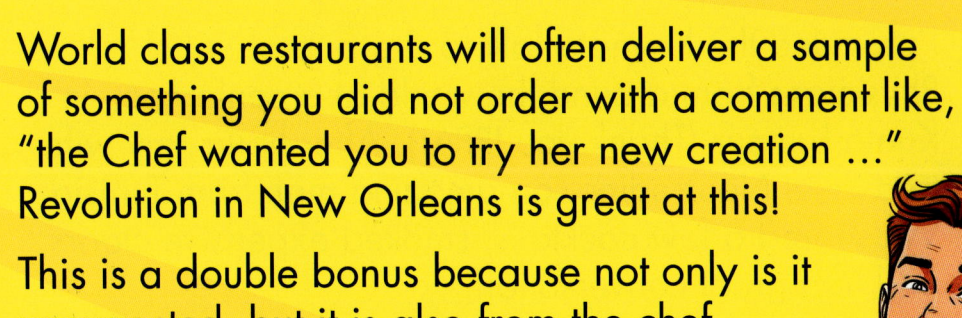

ALWAYS GIVE PEOPLE MORE THAN WHAT THEY EXPECT TO GET.

- Nelson Boswell

WOW LIVES IN THE EXTRA MILE

I provided the Keynote Talk to a group of Panel Physicians from around the world at a conference in Kuala Lumpur (Thank you IPPA!). After hours, my wife and I met Nourredine, an amazing man from Tunisia. We shared a few cocktails, smoked expensive cigars, and had great conversation.

He told the story of a man coming into a high-end club and ordering a particular brand of vodka. The man attending to his table disappeared and came back after a bit brandishing the vodka.

Later, the man requested another of the same bottle. The same delay occurred and this time the attendant was noticeably sweating when he delivered the bottle. The following conversation ensued.

108

CUSTOMER: "I NOTICE YOU TAKE A BIT OF TIME TO GET THE VODKA AND SEEM A LITTLE WINDED AND SWEATY WHEN YOU BRING IT."

ATTENDANT: "YES SIR."

CUSTOMER: "WHY IS THAT?"

ATTENDANT SHEEPISHLY: "SIR, WE DON'T CARRY THAT BRAND, AND I HAVE TO GO DOWN THE STREET TO GET IT FROM ANOTHER CLUB."

CUSTOMER: "I WANT YOU TO COME WORK FOR ME. YOU ARE THE KIND OF INITIATIVE TAKER I WANT ON MY TEAM."

I was the featured speaker for the annual meeting for QSC (Quality Service Contractors) and heard this great practice from a plumbing company. In the community in which this company is based, the people they service are mostly elderly.

After completing their work, they enthusiastically ask,

"DO YOU HAVE ANY LIGHT BULBS I CAN CHANGE WHILE I AM HERE."

Climbing up a ladder is dangerous for the elderly, so this little act of kindness completely **WOW**s their customers. AND, I am sure they tell all their friends.

ASK THE QUESTION OF YOURSELF AND YOUR TEAM, WHAT WOULD TAKE THIS FROM A 9 TO AN ABSOLUTE 10?

WOW PRESENCE

PEOPLE ARE SELDOM TRULY PRESENT. DISTRACTIONS ABOUND!

Research shows just having your cell phone on the table at a meal (even if you're not using it) results in your dinner date reducing the amount of attention they think you are paying them by 20%.

PRACTICE WOW PRESENCE BY ...

☑ Leaving your cell phone in the car

☑ Asking questions

☑ Focusing more on being interested than on being interesting

☑ Remembering something the person you are with has told you and inserting them in the conversation

☑ Great eye contact

☑ Paying full attention to what the other person is saying

JACKSON THE GREAT

My, at the time, 16-year-old daughter Callahan was dreading my gathering of friends at my condo that night. Even though it was a cool crowd of artists, business leaders, and others she hated to sit around and make small talk.

Then Jackson showed up. Jackson is one of the hippest and coolest guys in Dallas. He was a concierge for Barney's and now runs his own High-end Concierge company - Jackson the Brand. He could have been working the room, but instead he homed in on Callahan. He sat facing her for a long time fully engaged and attentive asking about every aspect of her life.

Jackson did not look over Callahan's shoulder to see who else he could be talking to.

He did not try to impress her.

He just showed up, fully engaged, sincere, interested in her life, her views, and her future aspirations.

To this day, when I mention Jackson, Callahan gives a sweet "Awwwwww" and says "I LOVE Jackson! Please tell Jackson I said hi."

HE MADE HER FEEL SPECIAL AND IMPORTANT AND SHE WILL NEVER FORGET HIM FOR THAT.

Contrast this **WOW** Presence with a store I walked into recently where the clerks had to finish their discussion before even acknowledging me!

PRACTICE BEING FULLY PRESENT. LOOK PEOPLE IN THE EYE AND TRULY LISTEN.

WOW FEEDBACK

We have become FEEDBACK MINIMALISTS.

I have seen performance evaluations reduced down to one word like "GREAT," "GOOD," "AWESOME."

This tells the recipient nothing.

The next time you give feedback put some thought in to it and be very specific in your details. Share things the other person actually did that you noticed or liked.

USE PHRASES LIKE ...

☑ "THE THING THAT REALLY STOOD OUT TO ME WAS ..."

☑ "ONE PARTICULAR THING THAT CAUGHT MY ATTENTION WAS ..."

☑ "I LIKED THE WAY YOU ..."

☑ "SOMETHING UNIQUE I NOTICED WAS THE WAY YOU ..."

☑ "THERE ARE AT LEAST THREE QUALITIES I SEE IN YOU THAT I WISH I COULD REPLICATE IN EVERY EMPLOYEE!"

"YOU LOOK NICE"
IS GREAT TO HEAR
BUT NOT NEARLY AS
IMPACTFUL AS,

"THAT TIE AND COAT COMBINATION IS GREAT. YOU HAVE EXCELLENT STYLE."

USE MORE MEANINGFUL WORDS!

WOW PHONE CALLS

- ☑ SMILE ON THE PHONE.
- ☑ BE CHEERFUL
- ☑ ASK "IS NOW A GOOD TIME?" BEFORE LAUNCHING INTO SOMETHING
- ☑ FIND OUT THE TIME FRAME THEY HAVE AND HONOR THAT
- ☑ CLARIFY BRIEFLY ANY DECISIONS THAT WERE MADE INCLUDING ACTION STEPS TO BE TAKEN
- ☑ SAY THANK YOU AND AFFIRM THEM IN SOME WAY

"I ALWAYS HAVE GREATER CLARITY AFTER SPEAKING WITH YOU," OR "YOUR POSITIVE ATTITUDE BRIGHTENS MY DAY."

BE THE KIND OF PERSON THAT PEOPLE WANT TO TAKE YOUR CALL.

SMILE ON THE PHONE. IT REALLY DOES MAKE A DIFFERENCE.

WOW MEETINGS

Meetings are boring. Meetings suck. Meetings take up a big part of a typical employee's day and VERY LITTLE is accomplished.

STOP IT ALREADY.

JUST STOP IT!

Meetings can be a valuable way to connect, collaborate, energize, spread the word, but they must be **WOW** meetings not snoozer time wasting, ego driven, boring droning on and on about stuff that doesn't really matter, meetings.*

"WANT A BETTER ANSWER, ASK A BETTER QUESTION." ??

"THE MORE BEAUTIFUL ANSWER TO HE WHO ASKS THE MORE BEAUTIFUL QUESTION." E.E. CUMMINGS??

*Read Patrick Lencioni's book Death by Meeting

DO THIS:

USE ACTIVE VS. PASSIVE QUESTIONS

Passive questions are characterized by being able to be answered by "yes" or "no"

"DO YOU HAVE ANY QUESTIONS?"

"IS THERE ANYTHING ELSE I CAN DO FOR YOU?"

Or, by presuming the response as part of the question.

SO, WE ARE ALL AGREED RIGHT?"

Active Questions necessitate a response.

"SEBASTIAN, WHAT IS SOMETHING WE MAY HAVE MISSED THAT COULD DERAIL THIS PROJECT?"

"KAT, WHAT IS ONE THING WE COULD DO THAT WOULD HELP ADDRESS THIS ISSUE MORE FULLY?"

THIS ONE QUESTION CHANGED EVERYTHING.

A hotel chain had a practice of calling up their guest at the end of their stay. This is how that call went.

HOTEL: "HOW WAS YOUR STAY?"

GUEST: "GREAT THANK YOU."

They discovered that this approach was offering almost **NO** usable responses or information.

THEN THEY CHANGED THE QUESTION.

HOTEL: "WHAT IS ONE THING WE COULD HAVE DONE TO MAKE YOUR STAY EVEN BETTER?"

This question brought with it a flood of responses yielding multiple actionable suggestions both minor and major.

Think about it. With the first question, most people wouldn't want to bring up the stale rolls at an otherwise great dinner. It would sound whiney.

The new question opened the door wide for feedback which was the whole point of the exercise in the first place.

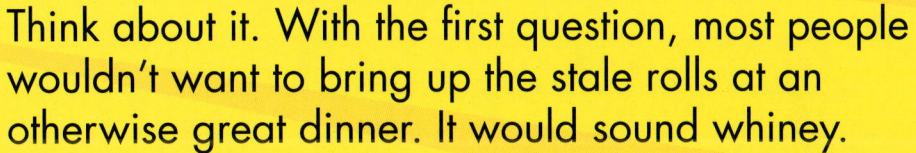

"DAREN MARTIN CHANGED THE TRAJECTORY OF OUR COMPANY. WE WOULD NOT BE WHERE WE ARE TODAY WITHOUT DAREN MARTIN, INCLUDING A NEW REINVENTED, REINVIGORATED COMPANY AND 4X REVENUE GROWTH IN 7 YEARS."

Bruce Sammis,CEO | Lockton Dunning Benefits

So what sparked that kind of praise from one of the most successful leaders in his industry?

Years ago, we were sitting in Bruce's office. He was frustrated. A competitor had just launched a bold new market strategy—something innovative and unexpected—and his team was scrambling to keep up.

After listening carefully, I asked him a single question:

"Bruce, I guess the question I would be asking is: What kind of company do we need to create where we're the ones coming up with the idea in the first place?"

THAT ONE QUESTION SHIFTED EVERYTHING.

It reframed the challenge from reactive to visionary. It sparked a new mindset, a new strategy, and ultimately a new company culture—one that led to explosive growth in the years that followed.

BRUCE SAMMIS IN HIS OWN WORDS

To me the magic happened when we combined the words think/WOW.

WOW went from a description to an action. From looking backwards at wow events to looking forward (creating) WOW

think/WOW helped define exactly what we expected from our associates and gave our culture a way to show up in daily actions.

For example, during peer reviews of strategic planning, renewal meetings, and stewardship reports, we always asked one question: "Where is the WOW?" We wanted every client to leave thinking, "WOW, Lockton—well done." That applied to big WOWs and little WOWs alike, and we expected it in interactions with clients, partners, and fellow associates.

When we introduced think/WOW, we played the famous video of Tiger Woods chipping in on #16 at Augusta. We compared our business challenges to Tiger's situation—

his approach, creativity, and the doubt from others. As announcer Lanny Wadkins said, "I'd be surprised if he gets it inside DiMarco's ball." Tiger didn't invent something new—he solved a challenge no one thought he could.

When the ball took its final revolution and dropped in, Vern Lundquist simply said, "Oh…**WOW**." Then silence. "In your life, have you ever seen anything like that?" More silence. Vern didn't over-explain or dissect the moment. He chose one word— **WOW**—and we all understood.

START USING ACTIVE QUESTIONS WITH INTERNAL AND EXTERNAL CUSTOMERS.

WOW INTRODUCTIONS

"HARRY, MEET SALLY" IS AN INTRODUCTION.

My good friend and founder of Fly Barbershop, Ted Hoffman*, never introduces people that way. Ted introduces people by giving a description of the other person and adds some element of who this person is and why they are important to him.

From the very beginning, he builds a bond by being the connector of two people upon which he lavishes unique and specific praise. Ted also connects the dots of why two people would benefit from knowing each other.

TED'S INTRODUCTIONS ARE WARM, HEARTFELT, AND LEAVE ALL PARTIES FEELING GREAT ABOUT THE ENCOUNTER.

*Nickname trivia - TBox = Ted Hoffman because he taught boxing in NYC for 10 years

WHEN YOU INTRODUCE PEOPLE DO SO WITH A 30 SECOND HIGHLIGHT REEL FOR BOTH PEOPLE.

INTENTIONAL DELIVERY THAT WOWS!

⇒ WHEN PEOPLE WALK AROUND FROM BEHIND THE COUNTER TO GIVE YOU YOUR PACKAGE OR ROOM KEY.

⇒ WHEN PEOPLE GIVE YOU A QUICK EDUCATION ON A FEW ELEMENTS OF THE PRODUCT OR SERVICE THAT WILL BENEFIT YOU OR MAKE YOUR LIFE EASIER.

⇒ WHEN PEOPLE AFFIRM YOUR PURCHASE DECISION, SAYING SOMETHING LIKE, "YOU ARE GOING TO LOVE THIS!"

⇒ WHEN INSTALLERS LEAVE YOU THEIR PERSONAL CELL NUMBER IN CASE THERE ARE ANY PROBLEMS.

THE DELIVERY OF A PRODUCT OR SERVICE IS A TREMENDOUS OPPORTUNITY TO DELIVER WOW! AND MAKE IT SPECIAL.

WOW STORYTELLERS/DESCRIPTIONS

I was in Playa del Carmen at the Paradisus for Elite Meetings Alliance (a division of CVent). This was my 19th event in a row for them Speaking and/or Emceeing.

Seth Dechtman from the Speaker Agency provides many of their Keynote Speakers and was in attendance.

HANGING OUT WITH SETH IS A BUILT-IN ADVENTURE.

He weaves story after story that captivate anyone present. He talks with his hands, he uses facial expression, he paints these elaborate scenes where you feel like you are actually reliving the experience. If Seth describes a place, you want to go there. If Seth describes a product he loves, you want to buy it. Seth is a storyteller.

Great Customer Experience people are excellent **STORYTELLERS** and give **RICH DESCRIPTIONS**.

THEY DON'T SETTLE FOR TECHNICAL DESCRIPTIONS ABOUT A PRODUCT OR SERVICE CHOOSING INSTEAD TO MAKE THE PRODUCT OR SERVICE COME ALIVE.

DESCRIPTION 1: THIS IS A 2019 CABERNET RATED 91 POINTS BY ROBERT PARKER.

DESCRIPTION 2: THIS 2019 CAB IS ONE OF THE DEEPEST AND RICHEST CABS I HAVE EVER TASTED. THAT PARTICULAR YEAR PRODUCED GRAPES THAT WILL REMIND YOU WHY YOU FELL IN LOVE WITH WINE IN THE FIRST PLACE. PERSONALLY, I BELIEVE THE 91-POINT RATING BY ROBERT PARKER IS TOO LOW!

DESCRIPTION 1: THIS SHIRT IS MADE BY MACEEO AND SELLS FOR $$$.

DESCRIPTION 2: FROM THE WHIMSICAL AND EDGY DESIGN TO THE SUPER SOFT FABRIC, THIS SHIRT BY MACEEO WILL HAVE YOU FEELING GREAT AND ATTRACTING THE LOOKS YOU WANT.

DESCRIPTION 1: WOULD YOU LIKE THAT IN RED OR BLUE?

DESCRIPTION 2: ARE YOU THINKING RED OR BLUE? TO ME THE RED SCREAMS POWER WHILE THE BLUE CONVEYS A SUBTLE CONFIDENCE AND CALMNESS.

PEOPLE DON'T BUY ART

An artist buddy of mine was desperate to get to Chicago to do a restart on his life. I offered to buy some paintings of his to help finance the move.

I picked out two paintings based on his extensive earlier descriptions of each including the meaning behind them and the symbolism in each one.

When I told him the insights he provided was why I chose those two paintings, he remarked,

"DAREN, PEOPLE DON'T BUY PAINTINGS, THEY BUY STORIES."

I THINK THAT IS TRUE ABOUT MANY THINGS.

BECOME A STORYTELLER. PRACTICE USING RICH RATHER THAN BLAND DESCRIPTIONS.

WOW EDUCATORS

Educating the consumer so they can make the best purchase decision is a **BRILLIANT CUSTOMER EXPERIENCE STRATEGY.**

Diamond companies began doing this strategy years ago by using the GIA® system to educate potential diamond buyers on what to look for in a diamond.

- CUT
- CLARITY
- CARAT
- COLOR

It was a hot Texas Tuesday afternoon, and I was on the phone (pre-internet) sweating profusely shopping for a new air conditioner.

ME: "HI, I NEED A RHEEM AC UNIT FOR THIS SIZE HOUSE. WHAT DO YOU CHARGE AND HOW SOON CAN YOU HAVE IT INSTALLED?"

VENDOR: "$$$$ AND BY THIS FRIDAY"

ME: "THANK YOU"

I HANG UP AND REPEAT

UNTIL I GOT THIS GUY ON THE PHONE …

VENDOR: "BEFORE YOU HANG, UP LET ME TELL YOU A FEW THINGS YOU MAY WANT TO KNOW. MAKE SURE TO ASK ABOUT THE MODEL NUMBER OF THE UNIT BECAUSE CERTAIN MODELS WERE MADE IN X COUNTRY AND ARE JUST NOT AS RELIABLE.

"ALSO, MAKE SURE THE INSTALLATION PRICE INCLUDES THESE SERVICES BECAUSE SOME VENDORS TRY TO TACK THESE ITEMS ON AS EXTRA."

ME: "VERY HELPFUL. THANK YOU."

I called one more vendor and then thought, "What am I doing?!"

I CALLED THE EDUCATOR BACK AND GAVE HIM THE BUSINESS.

TO EDUCATE ON THE PRODUCT MEANS YOU MUST KNOW THE PRODUCT. GO BEYOND THE BASICS UNDERSTANDING AND KNOW THE NUANCES.

SIMPLE WOWS

Master the simple things, radically well. Sometimes, it's not about doing something fancy. Simply executing the basics in a flawless, thoughtful way can create a **WOW** moment.

Audit every customer touchpoint to ensure it's not just done but done exceptionally well. Pay attention to things like packaging, tone of voice, and the details of communication.

APPLE PACKAGING

I am an Apple fanatic. Their products are beautiful works of art and very intuitive to operate. It starts, however, with the packaging. My wife knows if a new Apple product shows up, she is NOT to open it. Why? Because, for me, unboxing an Apple product is a religious experience.

156

Contrast that with many other products that you must go to war with the package involving chain saws and blow torches (yes, an exaggeration but that is what it feels like), just to get to the "goodies".

think/WOW COMPANIES DO THINGS LIKE SHIP PRODUCTS WITH BEAUTIFUL PACKAGING, PERSONALIZED THANK-YOU NOTES, OR A SMALL FREE SAMPLE TUCKED INSIDE.

OVER-DELIVER ON THE BASICS. PACKAGING SHOULD ADD TO THE EXPERIENCE NOT BE A DETRACTOR.

WOW STARTS WITH YES

Every customer service encounter should start with "Yes!"

I don't mean you are committing to doing everything the person is asking for because at times, it may not be feasible.

However, when you start with …

"THAT'S NOT POSSIBLE," OR
"WE CAN'T DO THAT," OR
"THAT'S AGAINST OUR POLICY…"

… YOU SET YOURSELF UP IN OPPOSITION TO THE CUSTOMER.

160

By starting with "Yes!" I basically mean saying something that conveys you're interested in what they are trying to accomplish and will work with them to address their needs.

For example, …

CUSTOMER: I NEED YOU TO BUILD ME A SIDEWALK IN 2 HOURS.

YOU: THAT'S IMPOSSIBLE! CONCRETE WON'T EVEN DRY THAT FAST.

CUSTOMER: ?%#!

Contrast that with …

CUSTOMER: I NEED YOU TO BUILD ME A SIDEWALK IN 2 HOURS.

YOU: THIS SOUNDS REALLY IMPORTANT, TELL ME WHAT IS GOING ON, AND LET ME SEE HOW I CAN HELP …

CUSTOMER: WELL, I NEED IT BECAUSE …

YOU: HMMMM. THE CHALLENGE <u>WE</u> ARE FACING IS CONCRETE WON'T EVEN DRY THAT FAST … LET'S WORK ON THIS TOGETHER.

The first approach positions you AGAINST the other person. The second approach positions you WITH the other person.

MAKE 'NO' FEEL LIKE 'YES'. TURN LIMITATIONS INTO OPPORTUNITIES.

FRICTIONLESS WOW

I AM STARTING A BUSINESS CALLED ...

"I TRADE $1 BILLS FOR $5 BILLS."

It is very simple, hand me a $5 bill and I will give you a $1 bill back in return.

"Ridiculous", you say. "No one will want to do that."

What if I told you people line up around the block to make this trade?

If this was in fact your business, how FAST would you want to make this transaction?

LIGHTNING FAST! ▶

Now, raise your hand if you have ever waited for 20 minutes or longer trying to get a drink at a bar?*

THIS IS THE BAR BUSINESS.

Customer hands the bartender a $5 bill
Bar tender hands the customer a $1 bill
in the form of a beer.#

This is not just the bar business.

It is **EVERY BUSINESS!**

Think about it.

Have you ever left a product you wanted to buy on the counter and walked out of a store because the *checkout line was TOO LONG?*

*When I ask this from stage, 95% of the hands go up.
#In my case it would be a Modelo Especial. Bottle over can. Better yet, draft if you have it. OR a Kettle or Grey Goose Vodka Martini up with a twist (unless you have goat or blue cheese olives!).

It costs the store more than just $$$$.

After this occurring 1-2 times …

I WON'T GO BACK TO THAT STORE!

GREAT QUESTION!

SO WHY IN THE WORLD DO SO MANY BARS & BUSINESSES MAKE IT SO DIFFICULT TO EXCHANGE MONEY FOR THEIR PRODUCT?

Anything that impedes a purchase transaction I call "FRICTION".

GREAT CUSTOMER SERVICE …
ELIMINATES FRICTION

I DON'T WANT TO ...

WAIT IN LINES
FILL OUT MULTIPLE FORMS
CHECK IN, CHECK OUT
HAVE TO REPEATEDLY LOG IN
WAIT ON HOLD
GO THROUGH A RIDICULOUS PHONE TREE
ANTICIPATING "IT'S MAKING ME <u>NOT</u> WAIT"*

"INSTANCITY" (MADE UP WORD)
IT MEANS – THE SPEED OF WOW!

*Do you remember the Ketchup commercial with the jingle, "Anticipation, it's making you wait?"

amazon

IS KING at ELIMINATING FRICTION.

They make it SUPER EASY to give them $$$$.

▷ BUY NOW 1 CLICK

▷ FREE SHIPPING WITH PRIME

▷ EASY RETURN PROCESS

▷ EASY TO SEARCH FOR PRODUCTS

▷ COMPETITIVE PRICING

▷ CUSTOMER REVIEWS TO HELP YOU DECIDE

AND MORE!

168

CUSTOMER SERVICE ON THE PHONE

THE GOAL SHOULD BE TO …

- ☑ Quickly identify the problem
- ☑ Rectify the situation
- ☑ Get me off the phone

People who have to call customer service are already put-out by having to use their time in this manner. Make the interaction **QUICK**.

It drives me nuts when I am bombarded with questions at the end of a call.

HAVE WE ADDRESSED ALL YOUR CONCERNS TODAY?

IS THERE ANYTHING ELSE I CAN HELP YOU WITH?

WOULD YOU BE WILLING TO TAKE A SURVEY?

RESPONSE TIME IS EVERYTHING

Customers hate waiting, especially when they're having a problem which is why they called in the first place. A WOW business doesn't just respond quickly; it makes customers feel like their problem is the top priority.

TRAIN YOUR TEAM TO RESPOND WITHIN A SET, ULTRA-SHORT TIME FRAME. EMPOWER THEM WITH TOOLS AND AUTHORITY TO SOLVE PROBLEMS ON THE SPOT, WITHOUT NEEDING TO ESCALATE EVERY ISSUE.

ENVISION A SUPPORT AGENT WHO NOT ONLY RESOLVES THE ISSUE BUT OFFERS A SURPRISE UPGRADE OR BONUS FOR THE INCONVENIENCE — WITHOUT NEEDING TO CHECK WITH A MANAGER.

WOW UNDERSTANDING

BEYOND BENEVOLENT OPPRESSING

"YOU CAN'T SERVE SOMEONE YOU DON'T UNDERSTAND. AT BEST YOU CAN ONLY BE A BENEVOLENT OPPRESSOR."

— Duane Elmer

Imagine you go through a particularly harsh winter and decide you want to help other people around the world who may also be suffering but without your resources.

You then decide to ship thick coats to people in Bangkok.

YOU ARE NOT SERVING THEM. WHY, BECAUSE THEY DON'T HAVE HARSH WINTERS!

174

Picture this! You have a sick friend, and you remember when you were sick as a child how awesome it was when your mom brought you chicken soup and hot tea.

So, you cook up some chicken soup, fill a thermos with hot tea, and deliver it to your sick friend!

Question: Have you served them?

Not if they don't like or are allergic to chicken soup and hot tea!

THE POINT?

DON'T BE A BENEVOLENT OPPRESSOR!

Great customer service begins with understanding the customer. If you don't understand them, even your best intentions could end up being oppressive.

WOW SERVICE DOESN'T EXPECT ANYTHING IN RETURN

HELP THAT IS NOT HELP IS NOT HELP.

I grew up in Bangkok. At the top of our street (It's called a "Soi" in Thailand) was a man with an intellectual disability who took it upon himself to direct traffic. People supported his very earnest efforts.

One day he saw my dad loading groceries and he came over to provide assistance. Dad tried to pay him for his help.

He indignantly refused, and said the very profound statement,

"NO! HELP THAT IS NOT HELP IS NOT HELP."

3 KEYS TO WOW
CUSTOMER EXPERIENCE

#1 LISTEN

✓ Pay attention to what they are saying as well as listening for what they are <u>not</u> saying.

✓ Resist making assumptions and presuppositions based on just a few buzz words that catch your attention.

✓ Listen deeper for what they are really upset about.

DIFFERENT PEOPLE WILL BE UPSET ABOUT A SITUATION FOR VERY DIFFERENT REASONS.

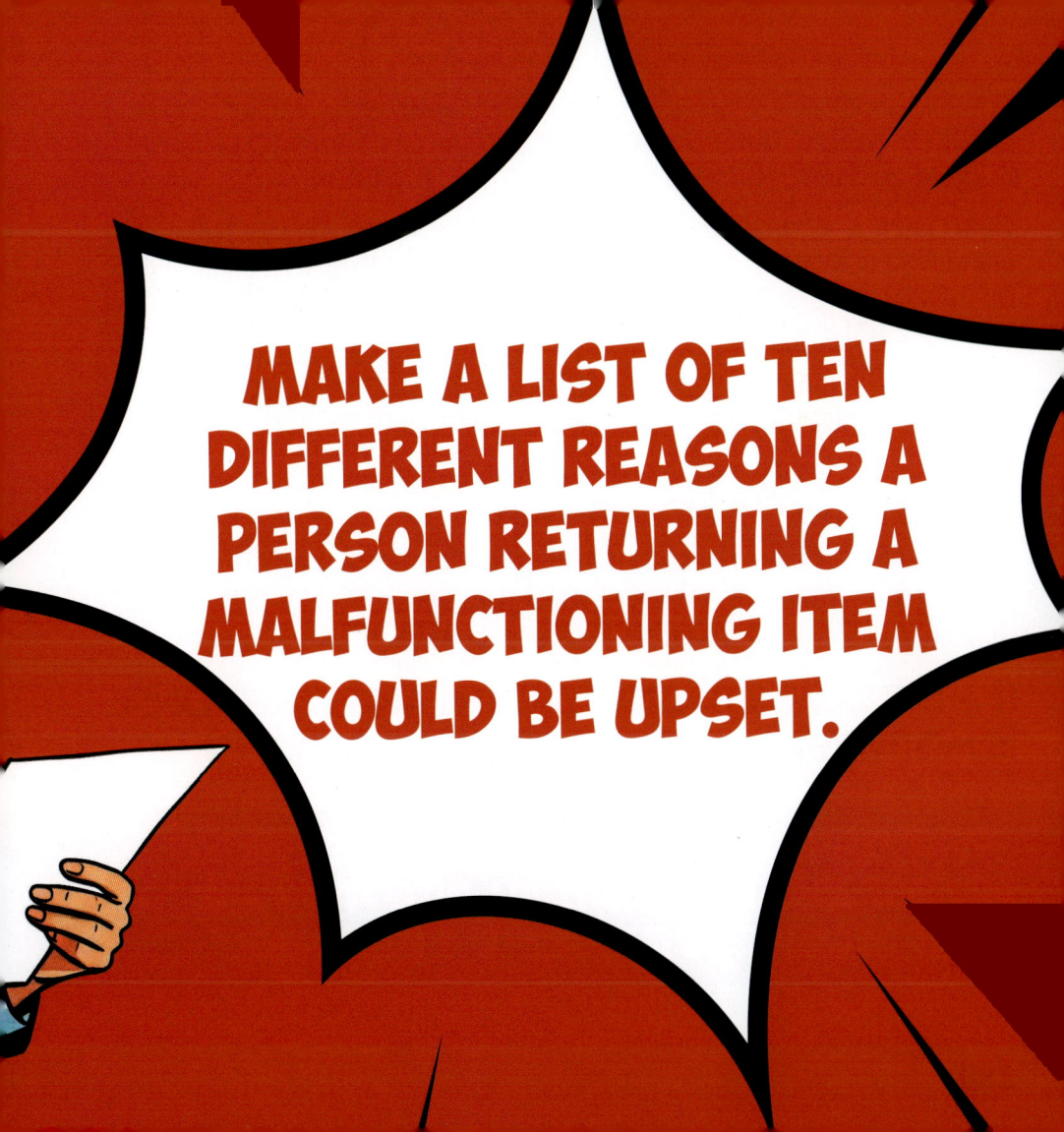

CUSTOMER SERVICE SITUATION: THE FOOD CAME OUT WRONG OR NOT COOKED WELL. IT TAKES WHAT SEEMS LIKE A LONG TIME TO GET THE SERVERS ATTENTION TO TRY TO RECTIFY THE SITUATION.

CUSTOMER A: IS UPSET BECAUSE THEY FELT DISRESPECTED BY THE SERVER'S SLOWNESS AND ASSUME IT IS BECAUSE THE SERVER IS DISCRIMINATING AGAINST THEM BECAUSE OF THEIR ETHNICITY, TATTOOS, LONG HAIR, ETC.

CUSTOMER B: IS UPSET BECAUSE THEY ARE REALLY TRYING TO IMPRESS THEIR DATE WHO SEEMS INCREASINGLY IMPATIENT.

CUSTOMER C: IS UPSET BECAUSE THEY HAVE LOW BLOOD SUGAR AND REALLY NEED TO EAT SOMETHING SOON.

CUSTOMER D: IS UPSET BECAUSE THIS IS THEIR SECOND BAD EXPERIENCE AT THIS RESTAURANT AND THEY ARE BEATING THEMSELVES UP SAYING, "I AM SO STUPID FOR COMING BACK HERE!"

IT'S THE SAME SITUATION BUT THE ANGRY RESPONSE IS MOTIVATED BY VERY DIFFERENT REASONS.

GREAT CUSTOMER SERVICE IS BEING DISCERNING AND NOT JUST LUMPING IT ALL INTO "THEY ARE UPSET BECAUSE WE MESSED UP THEIR ORDER."

#2 LEARN

✓ Gather as much information as you can about your customers.

✓ What do they like, what is important to them, what are their preferences?

✓ Implement what you learn into your products and customer experience.

Most consumers and customers WANT desperately for you to know about them so you can cater to them effectively.

In a live customer service experience, many **CLUES** can be gathered by simply **OBSERVING** the person you are serving and by **LISTENING** to what they are saying.

#3 LIBERATE

LIBERATE YOUR CUSTOMERS FROM THE TYRANNY OF …

✓ shoddy craftsmanship,
✓ tedious processes,
✓ complicated to use stuff,
✓ boring packaging,
✓ uninspired products,

WHAT ELSE?

In our quick read, high impact book, *The Sink: Leave it Better*, Co-Author Walter Nusbaum and I talk about "nullifying the need." This includes taking care of customer's needs they don't even know they have.

QUESTION FOR YOU: HAVE YOU ACTUALLY USED YOUR OWN PRODUCTS OR SERVICES?

This is a great way to understand what the entire experience is like – good and bad.

ASK YOURSELF ...

WHAT COULD MAKE OUR PRODUCT OR SERVICE EVEN *BETTER?*

ASK:

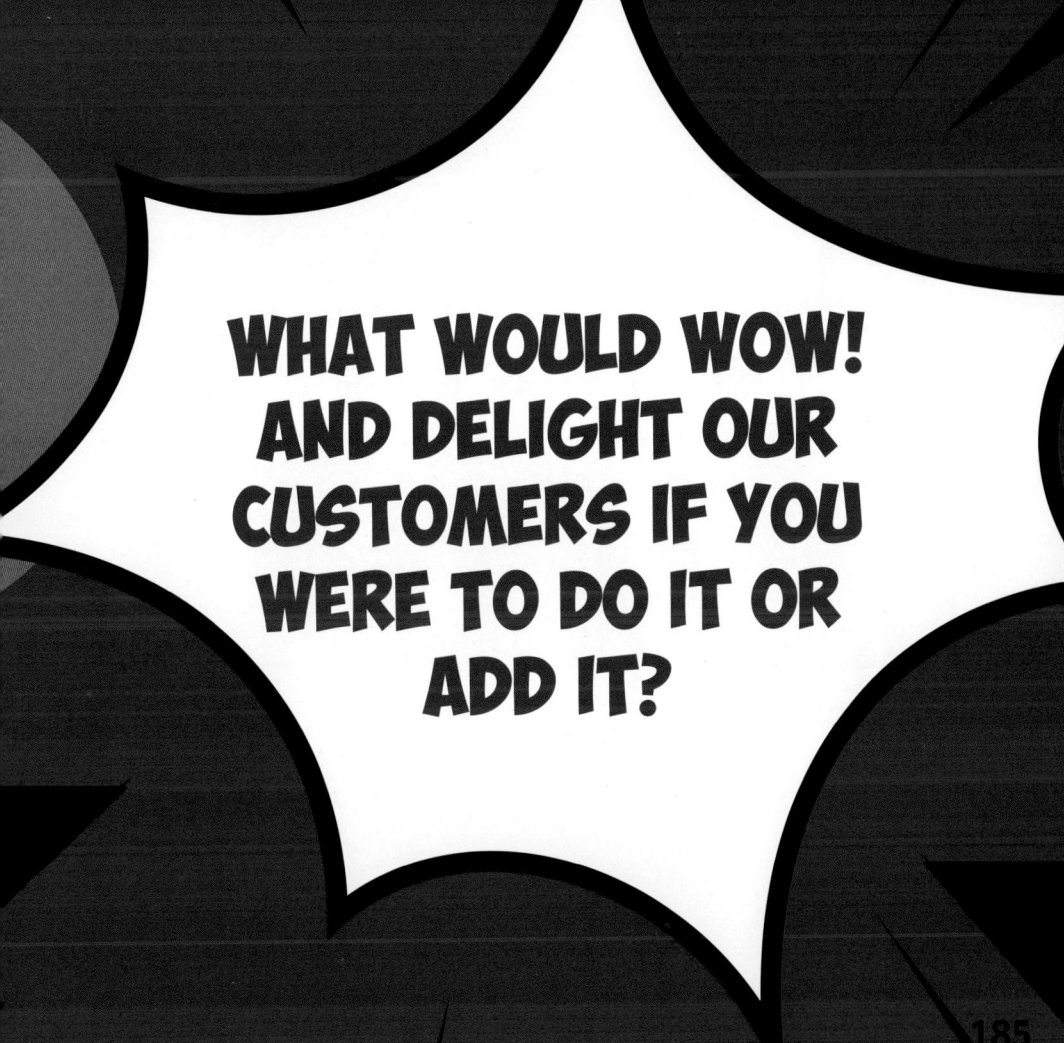

185

WOW JOB DESCRIPTIONS

WHAT'S YOUR JOB DESCRIPTION?

HOW ABOUT "EVERYTHING"?

Dr. Sung Won, a spine surgeon I was consulting, asked if I thought it was ok for the word "Everything" to be the first line on every job description for a new clinic he was starting.

I said "I think it is brilliant!"

I was emceeing a large Vistage event in Brooklyn when a frantic speaker said, "I am so sorry, I know it is not your job, but I really need a mic stand."

I replied, "EVERYTHING is my job. Let me take care of that for you."

SCRAMBLING IS NOT GREAT CUSTOMER SERVICE

"Customer service" based on a lot of last-minute heroics is not great customer service.

Many companies pride themselves on being able to "pull it all together" at the final hour.

Not only does this place a cloud of stress around the project, it also doesn't allow time for final touches and creative additions.

Fix the process so you are not running around with your hair on fire trying to take care of emergencies.

THE BEST CUSTOMER SERVICE IS THE CUSTOMER EXPERIENCE THAT NEVER HAPPENS BECAUSE EVERYTHING WORKS RIGHT IN THE FIRST PLACE

There is a reason Chick-fil-A provides consistent and superior service. Going the second mile is a part of their core philosophy as spelled out in this blog by Dan Cathy.

The second mile "ups the ante." It's the above and beyond. It's helping mothers with children to their tables, refilling drinks, engaging in conversation and opening doors for customers (at a fast food restaurant!) It's an authentic smile, and it is absolutely "my pleasure."

"Going the second mile means living out the Golden Rule and putting others before ourselves in a world that is all too often about 'me, me, me.'" Dan Cathy, Chick-fil-A*

THIS IS HUGE

*I ❤ their spicy chicken sandwich which I spice up even more by adding Texas Pete hot sauce.

IF YOU TAKE NOTHING ELSE AWAY FROM THIS BOOK ...

PLEASE ELIMINATE, OUTLAW, INSIST ON YOUR TEAM NEVER, AND I MEAN NEVER USING THE PHRASE,

"NO PROBLEM"

TAKING CARE OF YOUR CUSTOMER, SERVING YOUR BRAND WELL, PROVIDING GREAT CUSTOMER EXPERIENCE

BETTER NOT BE A ... PROBLEM!

INSTEAD SAY,

- ☑ "My pleasure",
- ☑ "Serving is my passion!",
- ☑ "It was my honor",
- ☑ "Made my day",
- ☑ "Delighted to help",

… or something similar.

OUTLAW THE PHRASE "NO PROBLEM" AND IMPLEMENT ONE OF THE ABOVE SUGGESTIONS IN ITS PLACE. BETTER YET, INVITE YOUR TEAM TO COME UP WITH AN ALTERNATE.

WOW IS ANTICIPATING!

ANTICIPATE – WHERE DO THEY NEED TO BE AT THE END OF YOUR INTERACTION.

ANTICIPATE - FROM THE BEGINNING WHAT THE DESIRED OUTCOME IS AND AIM FOR THAT.

CHOOSE OPTION ANTICIPATE

REQUEST: DO YOU HAVE A ROLL OF PAPER TOWELS?

OPTION A: GIVE THEM A ROLL OF PAPER TOWELS.

OPTION ANTICIPATE: DID SOMETHING SPILL? LET ME HELP YOU CLEAN IT UP (WHILE GRABBING A ROLL OF PAPER TOWELS.)

REQUEST: I NEED A NEW BATTERY FOR MY CAR.

OPTION A: REPLACE THE BATTERY.

OPTION ANTICIPATE: MAKE A NOTE OF AND RESET ALL THEIR PRE-PROGRAMMED RADIO STATIONS AFTER REPLACING THE BATTERY.

194

REQUEST: I BUY A NEW DINING ROOM TABLE AND CHAIRS FROM YOUR STORE.

OPTION A: YOU DELIVER THE DINING ROOM TABLE AND CHAIRS.

OPTION ANTICIPATE: YOU DELIVER THE DINING ROOM TABLE AND CHAIRS WITH A NICE NOTE ALONG WITH A FRESH VASE OF FLOWERS TO GRACE THE TABLE OR A BOTTLE OF WINE FOR THE "FIRST AMAZING MEAL."

ANTICIPATE THEIR REAL NEED OR SOMETHING THEY DON'T EVEN KNOW THEY WANT BUT WILL APPRECIATE.

ANTICIPATION IS SWEET!

It was Mother's Day in Dallas. My mom, being a Cajun from Port Barre, Louisiana chose Pappadeaux.

The server saw that I was out of tea. He also noticed the empty sweetener packet I had used

He deftly refilled my iced tea, selected the sweetener I had used, shook it down, and leaned it against the glass. I was dumbfounded by that level of attention.

I tell that amazing story often. I am sure that server is running a restaurant empire somewhere.

DEVELOP YOUR OWN "SWEETENER SHAKEN AND LEANING AGAINST THE GLASS" SIGNATURE MOVE.

WOW RESPONSE

SERVERS CAN INCREASE TIPS SIGNIFICANTLY BY DOING THIS ONE THING.*

*R. Van Baaren, R. Holland, B. Steenaert, and A. Van Knippenberg, "Mimicry for Money: Behavioral Consequences of Imitation," Journal of Experimental Social Psychology 39 (2003): 393-98.

CUSTOMER: "CAN I GET THE BACON BURGER WITH MUSTARD INSTEAD OF KETCHUP AND I WOULD LIKE EXTRA AVOCADO PLEASE."

SERVER 1: "GOT IT".

SERVER 2: "OK, SO YOU WANT THE BACON BURGER WITH MUSTARD INSTEAD OF KETCHUP AND YOU WOULD LIKE EXTRA AVOCADO? IS THAT RIGHT?" (SERVER 2 WILL RECEIVE A BIGGER TIP BY REPEATING THE ORDER)

PRACTICE THIS AT WORK WHEN DEALING WITH CUSTOMERS OR PEOPLE MAKING REQUESTS OF YOU.

LET THEM KNOW YOU HEARD THEM BY REPEATING BACK THEIR REQUEST.

REPEAT BACK REQUESTS PEOPLE MAKE OF YOU.

WOW IS NOT GOUGING

HAVE YOU EVER ASKED A SERVER FOR A RECOMMENDATION, AND HE POINTED OUT THE TWO MOST $$$$ ON THE MENU?

I have had this happen plenty of times. Does it make you question the server's recommendation wondering if they are just trying to drive up the bill and their tips?

I once had a bartender recommend two different glasses of wine only to discover when I got the bill, they were the two most expensive wines by the glass.

I was not a happy camper.

Servers and bartenders could avoid giving their customers this negative perception by one simple statement.

Something like …

"THE TWO ITEMS I AM RECOMMENDING ARE BY FAR THE MOST EXPENSIVE ON THE MENU. BUT THERE IS A REASON FOR THAT. THEY ARE BOTH AMAZING AND WORTH EVERY EXTRA PENNY!"

DONE AND DONE!

I would joyfully order the server's recommendation and welcome them into my circle of trust.

Versus adding the server to my "trying to take advantage of me" suspect list by them not acknowledging the high price in this way.

EXPLAIN WHY YOU ARE RECOMMENDING OR "UPSELLING" SOMETHING.

WOW RAPPORT

GAIN INSTANT RAPPORT WITH YOUR CUSTOMER

(REMEMBER, PEOPLE TEND TO LIKE PEOPLE WHO ARE LIKE THEM.)

Here is an amazing tool for making them feel great! Even on a first encounter.

The quickest way to gain rapport with someone is to

MATCH AND MIRROR THEM.*

*For more on this, research Neuro Linguistic Programing and Milton Erickson or, go watch my talk on Rapport at DarenMartin.com

208

MATCH: Matching is when you do exactly what they are doing. If they cross their right leg over their left leg, you cross your right leg over your left leg. If they talk using their left hand for gestures, you talk using your left hand for gestures.

MIRROR: Mirroring is when you do the mirror reflection of what they are doing. If they raise their right hand, much like in a mirror, you raise your left hand. If they tilt their head to the right, you tilt your head to the left.

When done subtly, both have a similar effect of increasing rapport on an unconscious level.

THERE ARE MULTIPLE BEHAVIORS TO MATCH OR MIRROR!

Are they talking fast, moving fast, and seemingly in a hurry? **DO THAT**.

Are they quiet, tentative, and talking slowly? **DO THAT**.

PACE – MATCH OR MIRROR THEIR PACE

 (can relate to speech patterns or body movements)

ENERGY – MATCH OR MIRROR THEIR INTENSITY

TONE – MATCH OR MIRROR THEIR TONE

BODY MOVEMENTS – MATCH OR MIRROR THEIR BODY MOVEMENTS

PAY ATTENTION TO THEIR PREFERRED SENSORY MODE

Need clues … the language they use will tell you everything you need to know.

AUDITORY: "THAT DOESN'T SOUND RIGHT." "WHAT I AM HEARING IS …" "HOW DOES THAT SOUND TO YOU?"

KINESTHETIC: "MY GUT SAYS WE SHOULD …" "THAT DOESN'T FEEL RIGHT TO ME." "THAT GIVES ME GOOSE BUMPS."

VISUAL: "CAN YOU SEE WHAT I'M SAYING?" "HOW DOES THAT LOOK TO YOU." "I'M ENVISIONING IT THIS WAY …"

THEN, match the mode they are using! If you respond to an auditory person with one of the other perceptual styles, you will not connect as deeply as you could by matching their sensory mode.

TEACH MATCHING AND MIRRORING TO YOUR TEAM.

WOW PROBLEM SOLVING

THE KEVIN S. DILEMMA

1. Kevin provides temporary housing (mobile homes) to people whose residences have been damaged in some way.

2. Kevin depends on insurance adjusters for referrals to his business.

3. Insurance adjustors are not allowed to receive gifts from vendors as this could influence their decision.

4. Insurance adjustors are a very underappreciated profession.

My Recommendation to Kevin was .... Put a fruit basket on the kitchen table of the temporary housing unit. Leave a card that says ...

Thank you so much for using our services. If you need anything or if everything is not perfect, please call me, Kevin at xxx-xxx-xxxx.

If everything is as it should be, please use the already addressed and stamped card I have provided to write a quick thank you note to your insurance adjustor thanking him/her for taking great care of you. - Kevin

UNBORE

(YES, IT'S A WORD 😊)

I worked with a company that sent customers large contracts to review and approve. I recommended they send the contract in a fancy box with a nice ribbon around the box.

On top of the contract would be a Starbucks gift card with a note attached saying, "I know these contracts can be tedious to look through, so I wanted to provide a beverage of your choice to make the process a little more pleasant".

I also suggested they insert an inspirational quote or joke in the sidelines of every 5th page just to make the review more fun.*

*Side Note: They didn't implement either of these WOW inducing suggestions. WHY? Because many people and companies are just too "busy" and/or nervous to be GREAT!

MAKE IT FUN

BAD WOWS

THESE ARE THE KIND OF "WOWS" YOU DO NOT WANT TO RECEIVE.

BAD WOW

"CUSTOMER SERVICE" ON THE PHONE

COMPUTER: "PLEASE ENTER YOUR ACCOUNT NUMBER. PLEASE ENTER THE LAST FOUR DIGITS OF YOUR SOCIAL. PLEASE SAY YOUR MOTHER'S MAIDEN NAME. PLEASE VERIFY YOUR DATE OF BIRTH. PLEASE CONFIRM WHAT YOU HAD FOR BREAKFAST THIS MORNING."

Finally, someone picks up …

REAL PERSON: "PLEASE GIVE ME YOUR NAME AND ACCOUNT NUMBER."

ME: "WAIT, WHAT? DIDN'T I ALREADY GO THROUGH THIS WITH A COMPUTER?!"

THE DRY CLEANERS

I got a call from a new guy at my cleaners saying he had discovered some mislabeled clothes of mine they had from 6 months ago. I showed up 2 days later to pick them up.

ME: "THANK YOU SO MUCH FOR FINDING THESE."

DUDE: "YOU'RE WELCOME! THAT WILL BE $26."

ME: "UMMMM, YOU'RE KIDDING RIGHT?"

DUDE: "NO"

ME: "YOU MISLABELED MY CLOTHES AND HAVE HAD THEM FOR 6 MONTHS!?"

DUDE: "WELL IT'S PARTLY YOUR FAULT BECAUSE YOU FORGOT THEY WERE HERE."

ME: "I COME IN AND GIVE YOU MY PHONE NUMBER AND YOU GIVE ME MY CLOTHES… "

DUDE: "I HAVE TO CHARGE YOU FOR THEM. ONLY THE OWNER COULD MAKE THE DECISION NOT TO."

At this point I am laughing because I seldom get mad at this kind of encounter. **Plus, it is GOLD for my writing and speaking. (You can't make this stuff up!)**

Even though they were right next door to our condo, we finally left this dry cleaner because they tore up so many clothes.

They were living proof of my maxim…

THE WAY YOU DO ANYTHING IS THE WAY YOU DO EVERYTHING.

BAD WOW

BRINKSMANSHIP

My friend told me that when she calls a certain Internet/phone service provider and gets the automated phone tree, when the machine asks what she wants she always says, "Cancel my service" because it is the only response guaranteed to get a real person on the phone immediately.

DON'T MAKE US HAVE TO THREATEN YOU TO GET A RESPONSE!

And while we are at it, why do the new customers get all the price breaks instead of your loyal customers who have been with you for years? I get the marketing aspect of attracting new users, but this seems shortsighted and unfair.

MARTINI GLASS

I was in Las Vegas doing a Keynote for an annual conference for Executive Assistants put on by Office Dynamics.

I was staying at the Delano which provided really great service. After my presentation, I went to the Michael Jackson tribute show with other conference attendees. It blew me away.

To celebrate a great day, several of us headed to a lounge for a night cap. Feeling the vibe of the incredible space with a spectacular view of Vegas, I went to the bar and ordered a Vodka Martini up with three olives.

The bartender presented me my martini along with a $$$ tab (ok, I get it given the context). This martini was in a tiny round glass rather than a traditional cocktail glass. When I joked with the bartender, "That is the smallest martini I have ever seen" he responded defensively, "It's 2.5 ounces!"

When I told our server later why I was switching to wine she said "Yeah, we don't use the traditional cocktail glass" with a look that seemed to imply my friends and I were out of the loop.

I said, "I have had martini's all over the world in some amazing bars, this is the first time one has ever been served in a glass that petite." The look on her face conveyed she completely understood and agreed but wanted to support the company's excuse for skimping on their drinks.

CONTRAST THAT EXPERIENCE WITH THE BARTENDER AT DOC B'S

who recognized my half full Vodka martini was warming up from the Texas summer. He deftly took it and poured it into a fresh glass which he had chilled by filling it with ice and then dumping it right before he deposited my drink into it.

THAT IS WORLD CLASS SERVICE!

BAD WOW

I grew up in Thailand in the 60's and 70's. American products were not readily available or were very expensive. As a treat, once a year, my siblings and I were handed the Sears and Roebuck catalog to pick out our one American toy for Christmas.

We would order 3 months in advance and hope it arrived on time because it had to come by ship. I would pour over the toy section for hours looking for the perfect gift.

One year I knew exactly what I wanted! It was this amazing helicopter that you could control as it spun around in circles. You could lower and raise it, hover, and take off and land. It came with soldiers holding their guns over their heads so you could swoop in and rescue them by hooking them. I could not wait. I posted the picture on my wall and waited patiently for that magical day when this perfect toy would arrive.

Sure enough, just in time the box arrived 3 days before Christmas. My parents knew we were desperate for our gifts from America, so they let us open the box early. My oldest sister reached in the box and pulled out her gift while beaming from ear to ear. My 2nd older sister did the same. My baby brother dug in the box and pulled out his amazing new toy.

Patiently waiting my turn, I reached in the box and felt around for my toy! I didn't feel anything. Digging deeper I felt a piece of paper in the bottom of the box. I pulled up the red piece of paper and read it. It said, "Out of stock".

I MADE A VOW THAT DAY THAT I WOULD PUT SEARS ROEBUCK OUT OF BUSINESS! IT TOOK OVER 40 YEARS, BUT I FINALLY DID IT!

A THINK/WOW COMPANY WOULD HAVE ENCLOSED A LETTER LIKE THIS ...

"Dear Friend,

We are so sorry we were not able to send the present you selected. We have enclosed a different but similar toy as a gift from us which hopefully will be to your liking.

When the item you originally ordered is back in stock, we will ship that to you as well. Merry Christmas!"

Your Friends at Sears Roebuck!

BAD WOW

TRASH PICKER

I fell asleep on the plane. When I woke up, I realized I had missed the drink service. I really wanted a cup of coffee while I worked on a book I was writing. I was sitting by the window and the two people between me and the aisle were sound asleep. I was stuck!

A flight attendant came by with a big trash bag. I got his attention and said …

ME: "WOULD YOU MIND BRINGING ME A CUP OF COFFEE WHEN YOU GET THE CHANCE?"

TRASH PICKER: WITH A HELPLESS LOOK ON HIS FACE HE REPLIED, "I'M JUST PICKING UP TRASH."

ME (IN MY MIND): "DUDE, WITH THAT KIND OF ATTITUDE, PICKING UP TRASH IS ALL YOU'RE GOING TO EVER BE DOING."

"IF YOU THINK HIRING PROFESSIONALS IS EXPENSIVE, TRY HIRING AMATEURS."

USING UNTRAINED VOLUNTEERS COSTS YOU MONEY

Stadiums and other venues are notorious for using volunteers to staff their concessions. My business partner and I waited several minutes in an unclear line watching a bunch of people wandering around behind the counter. The "unpaid/untrained" volunteers dragged around like a bunch of zombies not sure what they were doing or why they were doing it.

All we wanted was a Coke so when it became apparent this was going to be a 15-minute ordeal, we went elsewhere.

The revenue lost in the slow service and inefficient process **NEGATES** any profits you are garnering from not paying the volunteers.

GOOD
WOWS

THESE "WOWS" ARE PRICELESS AND ANCHOR YOUR CUSTOMER TO YOUR BUSINESS OR PRODUCT WITH SUPERGLUE!

REWARD LOYALTY CREATIVELY

MAKE REPEAT CUSTOMERS FEEL LIKE VIPS

Your most loyal customers deserve the biggest **WOW**s. Go beyond the typical loyalty points and create experiences that make them feel truly valued.

Surprise long-time customers with unexpected perks, early access to products, or VIP treatment. Personalize your loyalty rewards to make them feel special.

HEMLINE

My wife is a big fan of the women's boutique store Hemline. She is a loyal and frequent shopper with a significant part of her wardrobe coming from the New Orleans store located in the French Quarter.

She receives frequent texts from them notifying her of special discounts, new arrivals, sales, and more. They treat her like a V.I.P.!

239

SEWELL CAR WASH

SEWELL

Years ago, I bought a Lexus (now that's a **WOW** car) at a large dealership in North Dallas. One of the perks was free car washes for life. I then started working in downtown Dallas.

My car was dirty, so I pulled into the Lexus dealership on Lemmon confident in my "free car wash for life" sticker on my windshield and asked them to wash it. "Yes sir, we will take care of that immediately." 15 minutes later my car emerged all shiny and clean and I was happy.

The next week the dealership from where I had purchased my car called and asked where I wanted my tags sent.

ME: "I'M WORKING DOWNTOWN NOW SO CAN YOU SEND THEM TO THE DEALERSHIP ON LEMMON."

SALESPERSON: "DAREN, WE DON'T HAVE A DEALERSHIP ON LEMMON."

ME: "YES YOU DO, I JUST HAD MY CAR WASHED THERE."

SALESPERSON: "DAREN, THAT IS NOT OUR DEALERSHIP. THAT IS SEWELL, OUR BIGGEST COMPETITOR?!!"

MIND BLOWN. BOOM!

And guess who serviced my car for the remainder of the time I owned it AND who I was responsible for buying 3 more vehicles from, one for myself and two for friends? That's right, Sewell.

By the way, anytime my car was going to be there for a few hours they supplied me with a brand-new Lexus as a loaner car. Great way to introduce new models!

All it cost them for a lifetime of loyalty was a free car wash, great customer service, and not refusing me or making me feel stupid for bringing my car to the "wrong" place.

241

LEATHER MOLESKINE JOURNAL COVER

My buddy called and ordered a leather cover from a company called Holtz Leather Co for his Moleskine journal.

When the monogrammed cover arrived, it was the wrong size. He called them to apologize for ordering the wrong size and requested the size he needed.

CUSTOMER SERVICE: SIR, WE ARE SO SORRY, WE WILL GET THAT RIGHT TO YOU.

BUDDY: ARE YOU READY FOR MY CREDIT CARD NUMBER?

CUSTOMER SERVICE: NO SIR THERE IS NO ADDITIONAL CHARGE.

BUDDY: BUT I ORDERED THE WRONG SIZE.

CUSTOMER SERVICE: SIR, YOU CALLED US, AND WE HAVE A COMPANY POLICY THAT IF AN ORDER IS PLACED ON THE PHONE AND IS WRONG IN ANY WAY, IT IS ON US. YOU SEE WE BELIEVE IT IS NOT YOUR JOB TO EXPLAIN WHAT YOU WANT. IT IS OUR JOB TO MAKE SURE WE UNDERSTAND WHAT YOU WANT AND ARE GETTING YOU THE RIGHT PRODUCT.

THE COTTON HOUSE HOTEL IN BARCELONA

I finally entered the lobby of the Cotton House Hotel* in Barcelona tired from a long day of travel.

As I walked to the front desk the hotel representative said, "Welcome Dr. Martin!" I did a double take, but then got caught up in providing the necessary documents to settle in.

A few minutes later I asked,

"SERIOUSLY, HOW DID YOU RECOGNIZE ME AND KNOW MY NAME?"

FRONT DESK AGENT: "DR. MARTIN, I GOOGLED YOU BEFORE YOU GOT HERE. YOU ARE A WRITER AND SPEAKER, CORRECT?"

ME: "YES, I AM!", I RESPONDED.

I headed to the room with the promise the bellman would deliver my bags shortly.

*A Marriott Autograph Collection property

Moments later there was a knock at the door, and it was the guy who checked me in saying, "I didn't want you to have to wait on the bellman."

I thanked him kindly.

After he left, I noticed written across the mirror was an inspirational quote of mine!

THE WAY YOU DO ANYTHING IS THE WAY YOU DO EVERYTHING

— DR DAREN MARTIN

THE REST OF THE STORY

10 years later, as I am doing the finishing edits on this book I am finally getting back to the amazing city of Barcelona. I am now married, and my wife and I are going on a vacation cruise which ends up in Barcelona.

We will stay over there 3-4 days so I can show her all my favorites, The Basilica de la Sagrada Familia and other Gaudi creations, Picasso Museum, La Boqueria Food Market where you can get up to 36-month-old Jamón Ibérico de Bellota, and so much more.

And of course, we will be staying at the Cotton House Hotel!

GOOD WOW

JACKET AT OLD WARSAW

Many years ago, my former wife and I walked into a nice restaurant in Dallas for our yearly anniversary splurge. Our reservation was for 5:30 and at that early hour the restaurant was empty.

The maître d graciously took our names and asked us to wait just one moment. I wondered why we weren't seated immediately as there were obviously a lot of empty tables.

The maître d emerged holding a jacket and said, "Let me help you on with your jacket and I will show you to your table" as he deftly guided

me into the jacket. I apologized saying, "I am so sorry, I did not realize a jacket was required" to which he replied, "I knew you were coming; I went shopping today."

HE DIDN'T EMBARRASS ME.

HE DIDN'T POINT OUT THEIR POLICY.

HE DIDN'T MAKE ME FEEL LIKE AN IDIOT.

AND AS A RESULT, I HAVE TOLD THAT STORY MANY TIMES.

JUST FOR THE FUN OF IT, HERE ARE A FEW OTHER (FICTIONAL) "GOOD WOWS" AND "BAD WOWS"

GOOD WOW!: THE DOCTOR TELLING YOU THE HEART TRANSPLANT WAS SUCCESSFUL.

BAD WOW!: REMEMBERING THAT YOU WENT IN FOR A HERNIA OPERATION

GOOD WOW!: FINDING A LARGE SUM OF MONEY

BAD WOW!: LEARNING THE HARD WAY THAT IT BELONGED TO THE MOB, AND THEY WANT IT BACK.

GOOD WOW!: THE RESTAURANT DECIDES NOT TO CHARGE YOU FOR YOUR LUNCH.

BAD WOW!: THIS COMES AFTER YOU DISCOVER A FINGER IN YOUR CHILI.

GOOD WOW!: FINDING OUT YOU WON THE LOTTERY.

BAD WOW!: ALL YOUR FRIENDS AND FAMILY FINDING OUT YOU WON THE LOTTERY.

IF YOU FORGET EVERYTHING ELSE IN THIS BOOK (NOT RECOMMENDED) DO THIS AND YOU WILL BE GREAT!

TREAT OTHERS AS YOU WOULD LIKE TO BE TREATED.

Some form of this Golden Rule is found in almost every major religion and philosophy.

THE PLATINUM RULE is even better because it requires you to put yourself in the other person's shoes and serve them from their point of view rather than your own.

DO UNTO OTHERS AS THEY WANT DONE TO THEM.*

CHECK OUT THESE OTHER TITLES BY DAREN MARTIN

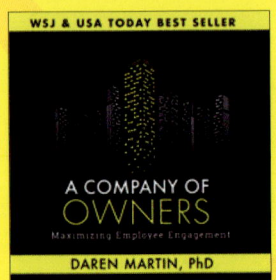

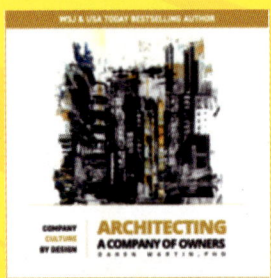

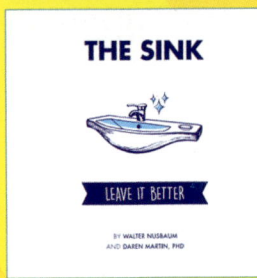

MANY MORE ON THE WAY!"

M DAREN MARTIN

Keynotes | Team Training | Executive Coaching
Strategy Sessions | Workshops
www.DarenMartin.com

Top Tier Advisors | Projects | Reinventions
www.TheTenzingGroup.com

Resources | Tools | Networking | Training
www.GlobalCompanyCultureAssociation.com

DAREN MARTIN, PHD
THE CULTURE ARCHITECT

Global Speaker | WSJ & USA Today Bestselling Author | Trusted Advisor

When you bring in **Daren Martin, PhD**, you're not just hiring a keynote speaker, coach, or consultant — you're investing in **measurable change that sticks**.

- **Your leaders level up.** They walk away with strategies they actually remember — and apply — to influence more effectively, lead with confidence, and accelerate their careers.

- **Your culture transforms.** Silos break down, teams align, and energy shifts as culture becomes your organization's greatest competitive advantage.

- **Your business grows**. Whether you're a global powerhouse or a fast-scaling startup, you'll see fresh momentum, stronger collaboration, and measurable results.

With Daren, you don't just get inspiration — you get **lasting impact.** The kind that elevates your people, fuels your culture, and drives your business forward.

Executive Strategy Sessions & Retreats | Keynote Speaking Training Business Advising | Leadership Development

YOUR TURN:

WHAT HAVE YOU EXPERIENCED?

SEND ME A WOW
CUSTOMER EXPERIENCE.
I WOULD LOVE TO HEAR IT!

CONTACT ME AT

DAREN@DARENMARTIN.COM

@DARENMARTIN